the Vowels

Written & Illustrated by
Jolie Canoli

Pronunciation Guide

A as in ant /ă/
A as in acorn /ā/
A as in father /ä/

E as in elephant /ĕ/
E as in teeth /ē/

I as in ick /ĭ/
I as in hi /ī/
I as in ski /ē/
I as in onion /y/

O as in opera /ŏ/
O as in old /ō/
O as in do /ö/

U as in up /ŭ/
U as in unicorn /ū/
U as in true /ü/

Y as in yes /y/
Y as in gym /ĭ/
Y as in spy /ī/
Y as in happy /ē/

Download the free Vowel Song here:

joliecanoli.com/phonics-song

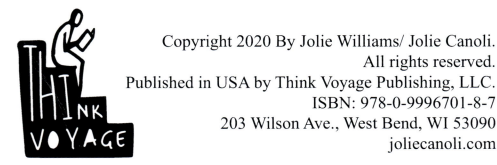

Copyright 2020 By Jolie Williams/ Jolie Canoli.
All rights reserved.
Published in USA by Think Voyage Publishing, LLC.
ISBN: 978-0-9996701-8-7
203 Wilson Ave., West Bend, WI 53090
joliecanoli.com

Welcome to Jolie Canoli Phonics: The Vowels!

Learn by seeing, hearing, and drawing. This book helps visual and auditory learners with foundational phonics crucial to learning to read and spell. Inspired by the Orton-Gillingham method, this book covers the 5 vowels and letter Y, their corresponding sounds, and spelling rules for silent 'E'. Learning these sounds lays the groundwork for understanding the structure of the English language.

Read this book aloud! This book is meant to be seen and heard. Each vowel sound has a short story accompanied by a visual icon. These images are carefully designed to help your child form a mental memory picture of the letter and its corresponding sound. At the end of each vowel section is a review page indicated by the uppercase letter with all of the vowel's sound icons. Encourage your child to point to each icon and say each sound on this page. There is a chant provided for you to say the sounds together.

Trace each letter. After learning the sounds of a vowel, a page is provided to practice handwriting. Starting at the green dot, have your child trace the letter with her finger, following the arrows, and ending at the red dot.

Free song! Download the free Vowel Song. Music is scientifically proven to aid in memorization. Plus, it's fun!

Learn the markings. Each of the five primary vowels 'say their letter names' (also known as the long sound), as indicated by the vowel with a line over the top (/ā/). When a vowel makes its soft sound, such as the sound 'a' in the word cat, the vowel will have a smile over top (/ă/). Some vowels have a third or fourth sound. For the third sound the vowel will have an umlaut. (/ä/) Fourth sounds can be found in other vowel pronunciations, so they will be indicated by previous letter markings. See the pronunciation guide for help.

Yodeling, hooting, and yelling resounds!
Vowels form words
with their musical sounds.

Dirty and dusty from working all day,
Give them a bath
and then learn what they say.

Draw them then clean them,
and they'll feel like new.

Welcome the vowels! AEIOU

A will say /ă/, the adorable ant.

A will say /ā/ like an acorn you plant.

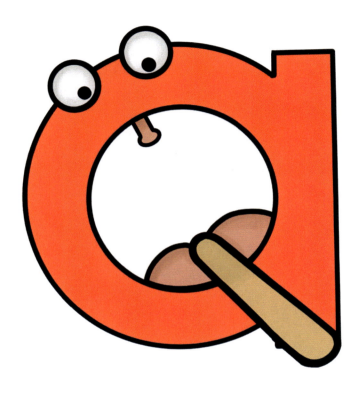

A can say /ä/ like the sound in "blah blah!"
Doctors will say "open wide and say 'Ah!'"

/ă-ā-ä/, /ă-ā-ä/
Let's all say it!
/ă-ā-ä/

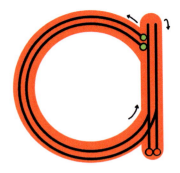

Splashing and washing
and wally wag woo!
Taking a bath, AEIOU.

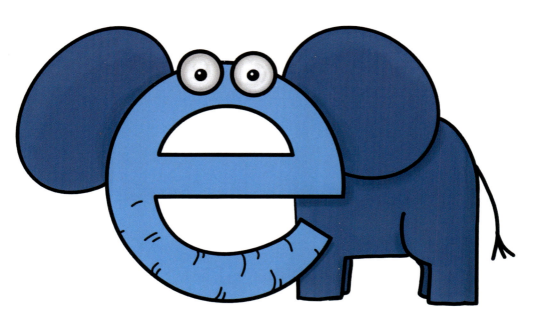

E trumpets /ĕ/ with an elephant trunk.
E shows his teeth,
smiling /ē/ with some spunk.

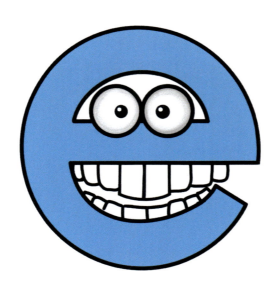

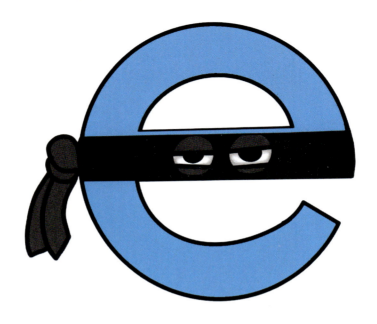

Shh! It's a ninja! The unspoken E.
Sneakily helping new words come to be!

Ninja ends words and it changes the game,
Helping a vowel to say its own name.

E takes a kit, then he turns it to kite.
E hops in cap, making cape take to flight.

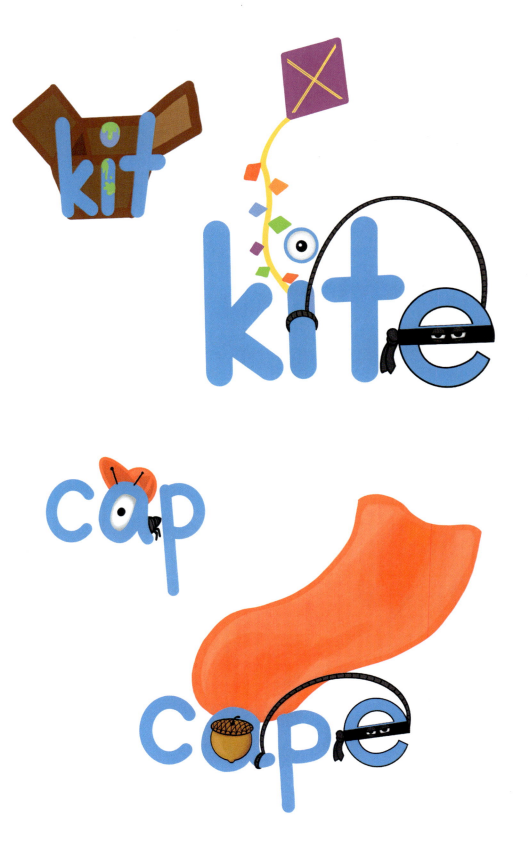

Words cannot end in a U or a V.

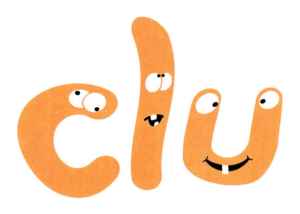

Jump into love! Solve the clue, ninja E!

Syllables must have a vowel, you see.
Follow this rule with the help of an E!

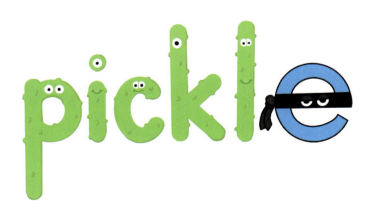

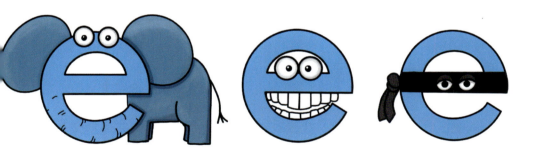

/ĕ-ē/, /ĕ-ē/
Let's all say it!
/ĕ-ē/

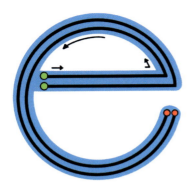

Squeegee and squeaky,
step sneakily through.
Taking a bath, AEIOU!

I says an /ĭ/
when in icky wet goo.

I will say /ī/
when he's looking at you!

I will say /ē/
when he's skiing on by.

I when in onion says /y/ like a Y.

/ĭ-ī-ē-y/, /ĭ-ī-ē-y/,
Let's all say it!
/ĭ-ī-ē-y/

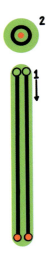

Wiggly giggly
dripping like goo,
Splish and a splash, AEIOU!

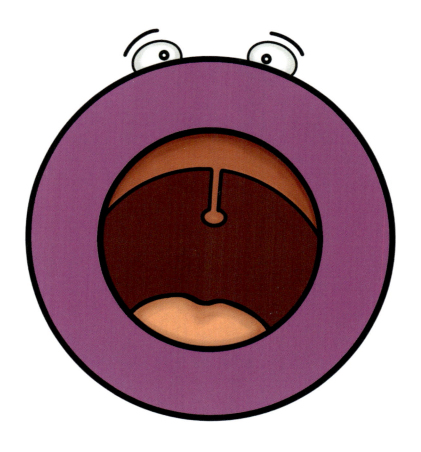

O sings out /ŏ/ like it's singing a song.
Open your mouth, and then sing right along!

Oh me! And oh my! Letter O is so old.
This grandma of letters says /ō/, I am told.

This round letter O will be hooting a tune,
An owl saying /ö/ looking up at the moon.

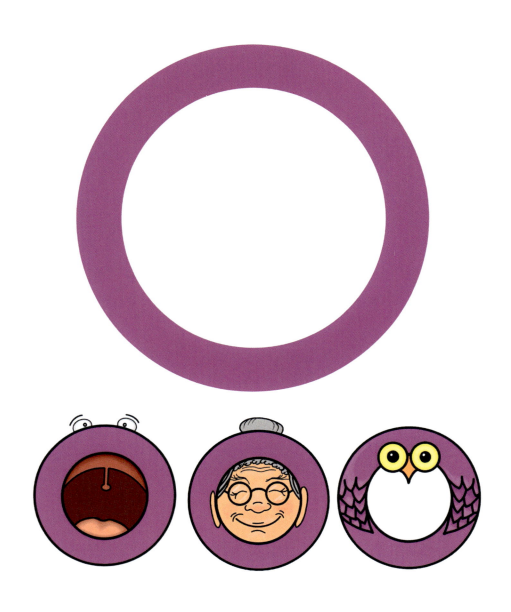

/ŏ-ō-ö/, /ŏ-ō-ö/
Let's all say it!
/ŏ-ō-ö/

Sloshing and sploshing and splooshing—
woo hoo!
Flop in the bath, AEIOU.

U's looking up!
He looks up to the skies.
Saying /ŭ/
as he ponders and
thoughtfully sighs.

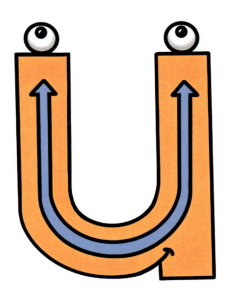

Unicorn U
is unusually tame,
Prancing in horseshoes
while saying her name.

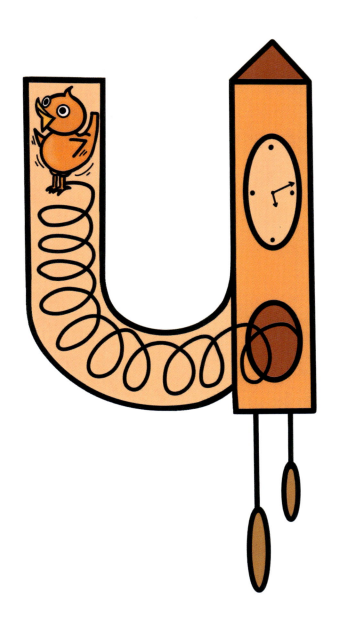

U can be cuckoo, it's true! Have you heard?
U will say /ü/ like a cuckoo clock bird.

/ŭ-ū-ü/, /ŭ-ū-ü/,
Let's all say it!
/ŭ-ū-ü/

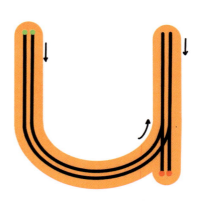

Gurgling bubbling
blutherering blue!
Scrub-a-dub-dub, AEIOU!

Why is a Y in this book? Aren't we through?
Sometimes the Y is a vowel. It's true!
This yodeling yak is the consonant Y.
But Y also sounds like an E and an I.

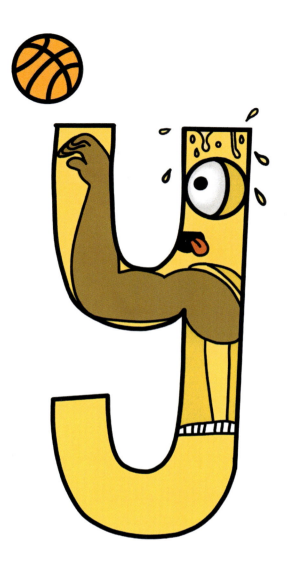

Y will say /ĭ/ when he plays in the gym,
Dripping his icky wet sweat on the rim.

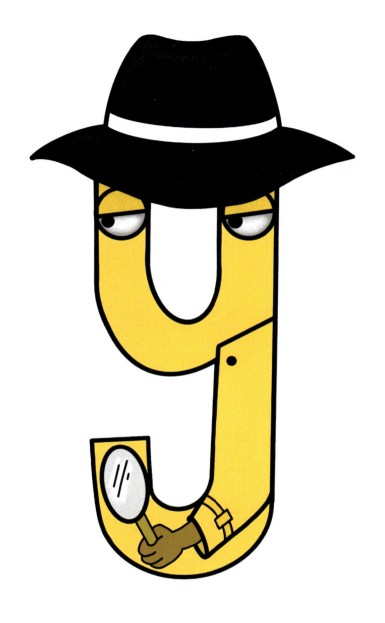

Y is a spy saying /ī/ as he looks,
Finding the clues as he sneaks in your books.

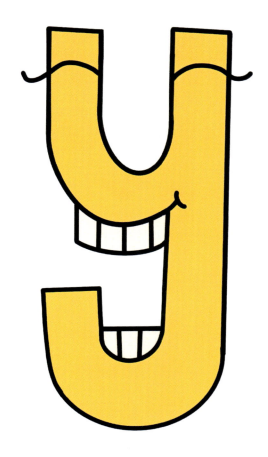

Y can be happy and clappy and free.
Smiling so wide, she's the Y that says E!

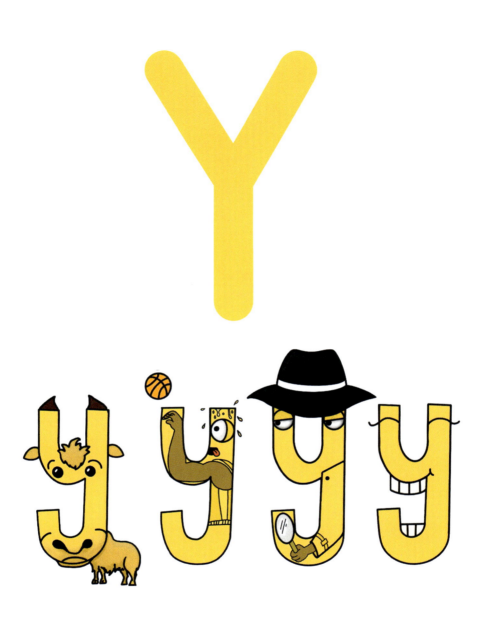

/y-ĭ-ī-ē/, /y-ĭ-ī-ē/
Let's all say it!
/y-ĭ-ī-ē/

Yodeling yelling,
and yipee ki-yay!
AEIOU and a Y
in the spray!

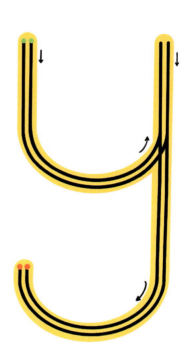

Well now you all know
every sound of the vowels!
They're clean, and they're fresh,
and they're drying in towels.

You'll meet them again
in your books when you read.
Farewell, friendly vowels.
We'll meet soon, guaranteed!

Made in the USA
Columbia, SC
17 November 2020